MORE of a Good Thing

Marriage Enrichment Exercises for Christian Couples

by Stephen J. Carter and Charles W. McKinney

CONCORDIA®
Publishing House
St. Louis

Copyright © 1982
Concordia Publishing House
3558 South Jefferson Avenue
St. Louis, Missouri 63118

Printed in the United States of America

Library of Congress Cataloging in Publication Data

Carter, Stephen J., 1941-
More of a good thing.

Sequel to: Keeping a good thing going.
1. Marriage. 2. Group relations training.
I. McKinney, Charles W., 1931- . II. Title.
HQ734.C3318 306.8 81-5395
ISBN 0-570-03840-5 AACR2

---

1 2 3 4 5 6 7 8 9 10 CPC 91 90 89 88 87 86 85 84 83 82

Contents

Preface

What is the church doing to help strengthen marriage and family life in today's world? Too often the church's role is limited to a pastor's sermon on Mother's Day and some occasional articles in the monthly newsletter. Yet the amount of crisis marriage and family counseling is rising at an alarming rate. Marriages continue to break up and divorced couples remarry, often combining children from previous marriages into a new family setting. Television and movies reflect the changing moral standards and the radically different life-styles created by a breakdown of the marriage and family relationships intended by God in His marvelous creation plan.

Do churches and Christian couples have to sit back and helplessly watch this destructive process take place in our modern world? We believe the answer is a resounding "NO!" Rather than curse the darkness, we would like to light a small candle with this book, *More of a Good Thing*. It is intended as a follow-up to our first marriage enrichment workbook, *Keeping a Good Thing Going,* originally published in 1979. A thirteen-session course for small groups of three or four Christian couples, *More of a Good Thing* is designed to help Christian couples share on the basis of God's Word and their marriage experiences some practical ways of strengthening their marriage. Couples will have an opportunity to communicate more effectively on a feeling level and to hold each other accountable for growth in specific areas of marriage.

This book should fill a special need for small group marriage enrichment. Excellent materials are available for large group family education in the form of films, filmstrips, and lecture materials. An abundance of fine books and tapes are also on the market for individual marriage and family growth in the home. Marriage enrichment retreats are provided nationwide with a variety of helpful approaches, ranging from totally couple-centered to entirely group-centered. *More of a Good Thing* will follow the format of our previous book and provide a follow-up experience for couples who have gone to a marriage enrichment retreat and want to continue growing in their marriage communication skills. It is targeted for use by couples in a local church under the supervision of their pastor as part of the marriage and family ministry of that local church. This small couples' group approach will blend effectively with regular worship, ongoing Bible study, and other marriage and family programs in the church. Couples who have used our first book *Keeping a Good Thing Going* may be looking for similar exercises with a marriage enrichment focus to use in their small group. We have received reports that our first book has also been used for other purposes, such as a supplement to marriage counseling, as a private discussion tool in the home, and as a resource for Sunday morning Bible Class.

These marriage enrichment exercises have been developed out of our marriage enrichment ministry at St. John's Lutheran Church, Peru, Ind. Charles and Shirley

McKinney, and Gail (Carter) and I have been part of separate small couples' groups in our church since 1975. We continue to grow, struggle, experiment, and adapt to the ongoing needs of our own marriages and of other couples at St. John's. We have no final answers or fail-safe techniques which will guarantee a successful group experience. But we believe firmly that when couples come together with an openness to each other and to God's Spirit working through His Word, Jesus Christ will become more real to the group, and each marriage will grow according to God's plan. To that end, we dedicate this new thirteen-session course and pray that God will abundantly bless your use of it.

—Stephen Carter
—Charles McKinney

Introduction—A Starting Point

We hope you are excited about using *More of a Good Thing* to help enrich your marriage. Spending thirteen sessions with your spouse in the company of two or three other Christian couples promises to be a delightful and meaningful experience for the two of you. This introductory section is intended to get you started on your marriage enrichment adventure by supplying practical suggestions for a rewarding group experience.

YOUR GROUP

Try to line up two or three other Christian couples who have attended some marriage retreat or are interested in enriching their marriage in a small group setting. Three or four couples in a group seems to be an ideal size so that every person in the group can participate fully. Emphasize participation as a couple within the group, rather than sharing as individuals. With this focus the group will reinforce the importance of strong Christian marriages.

Decide on how often you will meet as a group. You will have to consider your own time commitments and those of other couples, but these group sessions should rate a high priority on your schedule of activities. If maintaining and building a stronger Christian marriage is really vital to your life, you will make room for your small group sessions. Many couples end up looking forward to the group meetings and wanting to meet more frequently. Your meetings should be scheduled so that all couples can be present. You need 100 percent attendance at every session. Attempt to meet about twice a month. This degree of frequency keeps a good flow of group continuity while not overburdening your personal time schedules. Weekly meetings work quite well if group members have the time. Monthly sessions can be helpful, especially after the group becomes well acquainted, but tend to be too infrequent for the building of sustained relationships.

Your group can grow closer together as the thirteen sessions unfold. If you have already used *Keeping a Good Thing Going,* this course will add to your momentum by dipping into some new areas in greater depth. If *More of a Good Thing* is your first marriage enrichment group experience, you can start slowly in the early chapters and gradually increase your level of sharing as the group gets better acquainted. Just let your group experience happen. Every group has a different chemistry and will make unique discoveries based on the needs and expressions of the couples in attendance. Always strive to be forthright in your sharing, expressing yourself at the level where you feel comfortable.

We want your small group to be centered in Jesus Christ, surrounded by the Word of God, and enriched by regular prayer in the group and between sessions. Your common faith in Christ will shine through in all discussions of marriage areas. The opening devotions feature Scripture selections for meditation, and many of the sessions also draw in additional Scripture references for discussion by the group. Conversational prayer is encouraged each week at the close of the sessions with group members joining in as they feel comfortable praying. You are asked to keep a prayer list of individual needs, pray for these needs during and between sessions, and report regularly on answers to prayer. Make sure that your group sessions are firmly anchored in the Word and prayer.

COMMUNICATION WITH YOUR SPOUSE

The sessions are designed to open up new channels of communication with your spouse. Both group sharing and private couple sharing time should aid this improved communication. We believe it is vital to grow in understanding and communicating feelings. So often we listen and talk only with our head and not with our heart.

Feelings are given to us by God. He Himself demonstrates both positive and negative feelings toward His creation. He tenderly *loves* His children. He *hates* sin. He feels *compassion* for the oppressed. He is *angry* over injustice and oppression. Jesus Christ *wept* for Lazarus and Jerusalem. He was *angry* at the Pharisees and the money-changers. He was *joyful* at the Cana wedding celebration. He felt *sorrowful* in the Garden of Gethsemane.

In similar fashion, we have a constant flow of feelings, waxing and waning in intensity. Sometimes we shout for *joy* and other times we sigh in *discouragement.* We feel *tender* and *romantic* toward our spouse. But at other times a conflict with our husband or wife leaves us feeling *furious, hurt, rejected, lonely,* or *isolated.*

Some of us have great difficulty identifying and accepting our feelings. Virtually all of us struggle to express our feelings in a helpful way that can be understood. God accepts our feelings as they are, no matter what the situation. We should be able to accept our own feelings and those of our spouse as well. Sometimes hasty words or thoughtless actions call for confession on our part. This course will give you an opportunity to share your feelings in a loving way and to listen more effectively to the honest feelings of your spouse. Our awareness of feelings will be especially important in this new course as we delve into conflicts and conflict resolution.

HOW TO USE THIS BOOK

Although this workbook could be used in various ways, it is designed to provide exercises for a thirteen-session course with an intended length of two hours per session. Each chapter includes goals for the session, devotional thoughts in the form of Scripture and prayer suggestions, group exercises, and private couple time. Effective use of the material requires each couple to have a copy of the book. You may desire to have your own individual copy for reference and note taking. Each couple is expected to read the introductory material prior to the session, but only the designated leader needs to preview the exercises in depth.

SUGGESTIONS FOR LEADERS

The use of this workbook does not require a trained leader. However, a previously designated member must serve each group meeting as the leader for that particular session. A small amount of time spent in preparation will make your meeting more meaningful and enjoyable.

Assuming that the whole group has previously agreed on a meeting date, you should give each couple a phone call as a reminder a few days before the meeting is scheduled.

Always mention the date, time, and location plus anything that the couple is to bring, such as Bibles, Cokes, or other items. As leader, try to arrive a few minutes early and arrange the chairs around a table. Make sure scratch paper, pencils or pens, adequate lighting, and any special needs are ready for the meeting. Start your meeting promptly at the appointed time, and do your best to end it the same way. Of course, the end of the meeting may be followed with refreshments and a time of visiting and fellowship if desired.

Practical Tips

The group can meet in homes on a rotating basis or at the church. The setting should be as comfortable and informal as possible. You could meet in a circle of chairs or sit around a table. Avoid the distractions of children's noise or other meetings close by.

Normally, allow two hours for each session. Hopefully, your schedule would be free enough to allow additional informal sharing after the session closes along with some refreshments. You should never allow the material to make you feel pressed for time. Enjoy the sharing without constantly watching the clock. The leader should preview the session and approximate the time needed for sharing. Note the time reserved in each session for private couple time.

Each session will differ as to the exact time spent on the individual questions. Certain questions will stimulate more discussion than others. The closeness of the group and their freedom to share will also influence the time needed for the suggested questions. The meaningful sharing by couples in the group is far more important than "covering all of the material." Nevertheless, the following guideline is suggested: Spend approximately 30 minutes on the opening devotional thoughts, fellowship prompter, and reporting on "Since We Last Met." The new topic for the evening should take about one hour and 15 minutes with 15 minutes of that time reserved for the private confession and discussion time by each couple. The final 15 minutes of the session should be used for talking about the next session, sharing prayer requests and praying together as a group.

In selecting your groups, consider the compatibility of couples, common interests, and family situations, but trust God to mold each group together around a common faith in Him and a sincere commitment to marriage enrichment.

Other Responsibilities

Several small but important responsibilities are assumed by the leader during the meeting. During both the opening and closing prayer, you should pray first, give everyone else an opportunity to pray, and then finish the prayers yourself. Similarly, you should be the first person to respond to each item in the exercise. This gives the other members an idea of how to answer. It also sets an example for them in deep and honest sharing. After your own response, you may go in order around the table or call on members as you deem best suited to the particular question. Try to keep the meeting close to the time parameters given, but take care that each person has ample time and opportunity to "have his/her say" on each question.

Remember, you are serving as a leader and not a teacher. Resist the temptation to answer and solve problems. The learning process comes from the sharing experiences. Do your best to prevent arguments and try to keep the meeting directed at the exercise. It is very easy to digress and get entirely off the subject.

Be sure and include any needs that have been expressed in your meeting in your closing prayer. This is your opportunity to pull the whole evening together and ask for and receive God's blessings. After the prayer, your final duty is to set a time and date for your next meeting and to designate a leader. It is important that this be done before you leave the table or meeting area.

The local pastor can keep in touch with each group through a contact person and is encouraged to guide the groups in the use of the material. Joint meetings with other small groups from your parish are encouraged from time to time.

Fellowship Prompters

At the start of each exercise, immediately following the opening prayer, there will be a fellowship prompter, designed to "warm up" the group. Normally, it is somewhat light in nature and could provoke some laughter and pleasant memories. Starting with the leader, each member will get the opportunity to respond in whatever length of time is required. Comments and questions from the other members should be encouraged since these could prompt more detailed and elaborate answers. This opening time needs to be free and loose and honest so that an atmosphere of warm security and loving fellowship is present. The atmosphere is very important as each exercise gets into more serious and controversial subjects when each member must be able and willing to discuss freely personal feelings and emotions.

Who Answers the Questions?

The sessions are designed so that the questions may be answered by the group members in any convenient order. In the first few sessions it would be good for the leader to read the question and be the first to respond, . . . then proceed around the table. Some questions may be more effective if they are answered in a husband/wife or wife/husband order, and this is certainly always a prerogative of the leader.

Most of the questions require a *response from each individual group member,* and these are designated by the letters **IG.** So, as leader, when you see an **IG,** you know that an individual response from a group member and open sharing is desired.

Sometimes there is a question that needs *one mutual response from the couple.* This is designated by **MC.** It indicates that each couple should have some private time together to develop an answer, or response. Then the single, agreed upon responses from each of the couples are to be shared with the entire group.

Each session contains at least one item that is intended to be *private* and for the *couple* only. This is indicated by **PC.** For questions with the letter **PC,** each couple should get away by themselves, complete the question in *private* and return to the group locale when they are finished. No sharing with the group is intended or desired.

IG—Individual and personal response.

MC—A response that is put together and agreed on by the husband and wife and is shared with the group as a single response.

PC—A response only between husband and wife apart from the group as a whole.

SECTION I

Going with God

Welcome to a new Christian adventure in your couples' sharing group! Some of you are continuing your marriage enrichment after completing our first book, *Keeping a Good Thing Going*. Others may be starting a couples' group with this thirteen-session course. This course is divided into four sections designed to lead you into a deeper and closer marriage relationship by exploring key practical areas of married life today. The first section—"Going with God"—will help you build group closeness, focus on the One who alone instituted and sustains marriage, and start addressing important marriage issues.

You begin with a session on "Marriage and a New Commitment." Each member of the group needs to make a commitment to this thirteen-session course—to be regular in attendance at meetings, to work on the assigned topics as a couple between group sessions, and to participate fully in the sharing. This course will go somewhat deeper than *Keeping a Good Thing Going* and group accountability will be essential for maximum marriage enrichment by each couple. God's steadfast commitment to you in Jesus Christ will provide the foundation for your new commitments to Him and to each other.

In Session 2 you will consider "Marriage and Christian Maturity." After a relaxed sharing on the maturing process in your family growth and development and a similar sharing on the maturing process in the area of material possessions, your group will discuss the personality of your marriage as an entity which needs Christian maturing. You will conclude this session by a discussion of your spiritual maturity as a couple.

Section 1 will conclude with a discussion of "Marriage and Confession." God offers you a tremendous resource for growth in your marriage through the regular process of confession and absolution. While most Christians understand at least with their head the importance of confessing sin to God, few apply this powerful tool to everyday living at home. With this session you will begin to practice confession with your spouse and also to assure your loved one of forgiveness by the blood of Christ. Private confession time with your spouse will then be included as a regular part of succeeding sessions. Not only is confession and absolution a vital ingredient for "Going with God," it also may be the most beneficial part of this entire course for your marriage.

CHAPTER 1

Marriage and a New Commitment

"I'm sorry I can't make it to church Sunday. I've got tickets to a pro-football game." "I would like to attend a marriage retreat, but I hate to leave the children, and we don't have the money." "A couple's group sounds great, but all of our schedules are so busy that I'm not sure how we can fit in the meeting times." "When I take on a new commitment, I want to make certain I can follow through instead of letting everyone else down."

All of the above statements relate to making commitments. As you will learn in this session, we have time for things when we feel responsible for them, enjoy doing them, and/or have a need for them. Marriage enrichment requires a continuing commitment of husband and wife to grow together. This thirteen-session group adventure requires a clear-cut commitment on the part of each couple in the group to follow through on attendance at meetings, full participation, carrying out assignments between sessions, prayer support, and couple communication within and outside the group. After getting acquainted and establishing your positive expectations and reservations for the group, you will explore the many commitments in your life and decide whether you want to make a new commitment to this course. Whether you are forming a new couples' group or are continuing a marriage enrichment experience following *Keeping a Good Thing Going,* this session on commitment is crucial to the entire course. Remember that God has chosen You in Christ, His commitment never wavers, and He will empower any new commitment you make.

GOALS FOR SESSION 1

1. Get acquainted or renew acquaintances with the other couples in the group.
2. Discuss expectations about this new group experience.
3. Explore commitments in our lives and rate the relative importance of this group experience to our marriage.
4. Make a new commitment to this group to complete this thirteen-session course.
5. Renew our lifelong commitment to each other as husbands and wives.
6. Endeavor to grow even closer in our commitment to God.

DEVOTIONAL THOUGHTS

(Scripture passages are read aloud by group members with time for meditation on each Scripture section.)

Scripture

Matthew 18:19-20—God's *promise* for your group.
Matthew 19:4-6—God's *plan* for your marriage.
Matthew 28:5-10—God's *peace* for your fears and *purpose* for your new adventure.

Prayer Thoughts for Session 1

(Leader prays using the following thoughts for a guide. In subsequent sessions, group prayer will be used with the goals for the session as a guideline.)

1. Enjoyable interaction of the new group.
2. Mutual commitment to marriage enrichment as a couple.
3. A new commitment to the thirteen-session course.
4. Presence of Jesus Christ in the group.

GROUP EXERCISES

Getting Acquainted—Fellowship Prompter

IG 1. This is my wife/husband ________ , and one of her/his best qualities is ________ .

IG 2. During the past year, what events or series of events caused you to laugh longest and hardest?

Discussing Expectations

IG 1. What do you hope this group can offer that will be positive and important in your marriage?

IG 2. What are some reservations you have about this new course and the group involvement?

Exploring Commitments

IG 1. We make commitments for various reasons. Try to fill in several of your personal commitments under each of the following headings and share your list with the group.

	Because I think it is my responsibility	Because I enjoy it	Because I need it
examples:	my job family reunions	my Monday night bowling my garden	Bible Study physical examinations

IG 2. Put your commitment to this group under one and only one of the above headings and tell why you made that particular choice.

IG 3. Discuss your commitment to marriage enrichment relative to your other commitments. What changes, if any, need to be made?

MAKING A NEW COMMITMENT

IG 1. Read through the commitment form included as part of the closing devotion.

PC 2. Couple Dialog—What new commitment am I willing to make to marriage enrichment and how does that answer make me feel?

MC 3. Group response—Each couple shares their new commitment with the group along with their feelings about it. How can God help us keep these commitments (John 15:11-17)?

IG 4. The leader should read aloud the commitment form and give each member the opportunity to affirm his/her intentions.

IG 5. Closing group prayer around the circle. (In the prayer include items for which you are thankful and prayer requests for the group and individuals. Keep a notebook on prayer requests.)

ASSIGNMENT FOR SESSION 2

IG 1. Reread the Scripture sections for Session 1.
IG 2. Read the introductory material for Session 2.
MC 3. Further discuss your list of commitments under the three categories and report back on any changes you contemplate.
IG 4. Pray for the group's prayer requests.

COMMITMENT FORM

I agree to become a member of this couples' group for the thirteen sessions. I also agree to give priority to my attendance at all meetings. I will carry out the assignments between sessions as agreed by the group. I will offer my prayer support for the couples in the group. I will also share deeply and honestly with the other group members. I understand that no effort will be made to embarrass me or to pry into my personal life beyond that which I am willing to share. Furthermore, I understand that everything that is said and heard here will be kept in strict confidence. I look forward to this joining towards a deeper and mutual relationship between my spouse and me and between my Christian friends and myself.

Signed ________
Dated ________

CHAPTER 2

Marriage and Christian Maturity

"We're in love!" When a dating couple or newlyweds make such an announcement, they mean it passionately and intend a lifelong commitment. But when a golden wedding anniversary couple quietly speaks the same words, they are filled with a depth of experience and a time-tested commitment that reflect the maturing process in a Christian marriage. Marriages don't stand still; they either grow or wither. Your couples' group offers a tremendous resource of experience to share about Christian maturity.

In this session you will have an opportunity to reflect on several areas of your marriage. Each person will be describing changes in the marriage over the years as a result of children, or others living in the home. Each couple will add unique variety to this discussion on family growth. Then you will have the opportunity to share your thoughts on the progress in material possessions with comments on attitudes toward these possessions.

After these preliminary discussions, you will try to come to grips with the "personality" of your marriage. Your marriage has unique characteristics which are different from either of your individual traits. Your marriage's "personality" changes and matures as the years pass. You will be asked to describe the "personality" of your marriage and see how it is maturing.

Finally, you will be challenged to explore several categories which help you to mature spiritually, including church attendance, Bible study, prayer, confession, etc. Your frank evaluation and commitment to specific steps toward spiritual maturity will significantly help your Christian marriage.

"We're in love!" Session 2 should help you fill those words with new meaning.

GOALS FOR SESSION 2

1. Reflect on the changes in your family, e.g., children's growth and development.
2. Reflect on the maturing process in attitudes toward material possessions.
3. Consider the "personality of our marriage" in terms of Christian maturing.
4. Commit yourselves to growth in a specific area of spiritual maturity.

DEVOTIONAL THOUGHTS

Scripture

Psalm 128—Family blessings from generation to generation.
Proverbs 30:7-9—A mature attitude toward material possessions.
Ephesians 5:21-33—Maturing in the marriage relationship.
Ephesians 4:13-16—The spiritual maturity process.

Group Prayer

GROUP EXERCISES

Getting Acquainted—Fellowship Prompter

IG Describe the time or event of your life when you felt the very closest to God.

Since We Last Met

IG Each person reports on any changes made in the commitment list that was completed at the last session.

Maturity in Family Growth and Development

IG What changes have taken place in your marriage because of children, and others living in your home?

Maturity in Attitudes Toward Material Possessions

IG 1. Tell about the progress of this marriage in material possessions. This should include the different places you have lived—cars that you have owned—your furniture and your jobs plus other important and interesting details.

IG 2. Describe any changes in attitude toward material possessions you have noticed from early marriage until now in yourself—in your spouse.

Maturity in the Personality of Your Marriage

IG 1. As husband and wife blend into the oneness of marriage, that union tends to develop a personality of its own. What one word best describes your marriage? Why?

IG 2. As you think about your marriage from its beginning until now, what differences do you notice in the "personality" and "temperament" of that marriage?

IG 3. What changes would you like to see in the personality of your marriage and exactly what are you willing to do to effect those changes?

PC 4. Couple Dialog—What quality best describes your marriage right now and how does it make you feel?

Spiritual Maturity

IG 1. Describe the changes in the spiritual maturity of your marriage from its beginning until the present time.

IG 2. Mutual and simultaneous participation in spiritual opportunities by the husband and wife greatly enhance the possibilities for spiritual maturity. In this context, how do you rate your marriage in the following categories? Rate each item 1 to 10 with 1 as the poorest and 10 as the best:

Worship Attendance	_____	Confession	_____
Bible study	_____	Communion	_____
Devotions	_____	Service to the Lord	_____
Prayer	_____	Mutual encouragement for some of the above	_____

MC 3. Choose the one item from the above list which you would most like to improve in your marriage. Tell the group your selection and why it was your choice. If you are willing to take this as a project, state how you plan to improve your participation as a couple in this area. Plan to report your progress at the next group meeting.

IG 4. Closing prayer around the circle along with reporting on prayer notebook requests and adding to the list.

ASSIGNMENT FOR SESSION 3

IG 1. Reread the Scripture sections for Session 2.
IG 2. Read the introductory material for Session 3.
IG 3. Be prepared to report back on the progress of your spiritual growth area.
IG 4. Continue to pray for the group's prayer requests.

CHAPTER 3

Marriage and Confession

Both Scripture and modern psychiatry stress the importance of confession as a way of dealing with guilt. As Christians, we are taught that God wants us to confess our sins of thought, word, and deed and that full forgiveness is available to us on the basis of Christ's death on the cross 2,000 years ago. We have opportunity on Sunday mornings to confess our sins with our fellow Christians in a general way as part of the service.

Nevertheless, we often struggle with guilt in our life, find it difficult to confess specific sins even to God in private but especially to a fellow Christian, and don't easily offer forgiveness to the other person even when they ask. Two of the most difficult expressions in the English language are "I'm sorry" and "I forgive you." Nowhere is honest confession and loving forgiveness needed more than in the marriage relationship where daily frictions and simmering personality clashes often lead to an extended cold war with little hope of a truce, let alone a peace treaty. Yet husbands and wives frequently do not know how to confess to one another and assure each other of God's forgiveness.

This lesson will introduce you to Scriptural sections on confession for your discussion, followed by an evaluation of the need for confession in your own marriage and a consideration of the road blocks which prevent a meaningful confessional experience with your spouse. You will then have the opportunity to spend some time alone with your spouse to confess sins that bother you and to receive the assurance from your mate that your sins are forgiven for Jesus' sake. In succeeding sessions, you will have similar confession time to correlate with the topic for that evening.

The following is a form for confession and absolution which we encourage you to use at this meeting and in succeeding sessions if that proves helpful to you for the confessional time. Sometimes we will encourage written preparation; at other times we will encourage private thinking preparation.

INSTRUCTIONS FOR CONFESSION AND ABSOLUTION

1. Couples meet privately.
2. Take the first few minutes for sharing your written reflections or for private thinking about your own sins that bother you in your marriage relationship.
3. Then—one of you confess (formula is on the bottom of this sheet).
4. The one "hearing the confession" is then to absolve, with the suggestion of making the sign of the cross on the forehead of the person being absolved.
5. Now reverse—the second person confess to the first, and the first person speaks absolution.
6. When done, give thanks to God for His grace and forgiveness in Christ.

Formula of Confession:

I confess before God and in the presence of you, my husband/wife, that I have sinned against Him and others. (Here you may add any specific sins that you wish to mention.) I ask God for forgiveness of these sins, as well as all those I have not mentioned or do not even know, and I ask you to assure me of that forgiveness.

Formula of Absolution:

As your Christian husband/wife, speaking by my Lord's command, I remind you of God's grace to you in Jesus Christ, and I assure you of God's forgiveness for all your sins in the name of the Father and of the Son and of the Holy Spirit. Amen.

GOALS FOR SESSION 3

1. Investigate together some pertinent Scripture passages on confession and absolution.
2. Discuss the need for confession in our marriage.
3. Examine some of the roadblocks which prevent a meaningful confessional life at home.
4. Experience some personal confessional time as a couple and reflect with the group on the results of that sharing time.

DEVOTIONAL THOUGHTS

Scripture

Psalm 32:1-5—The Blessings of Honest Confession.
1 John 1:9—The Promise of Forgiveness.
James 5:16—The Command to Confess Our Sins to Each Other.
Ephesians 4:32—The Command to Forgive Each Other and Love One Another.

Group Prayer

GROUP EXERCISES

Getting Acquainted—Fellowship Prompter

IG Tell about the happiest person you know and what makes him/her that way.

Since We Last Met

IG Each person reports on his spiritual growth since the last session. This should include the *area* (prayer, Bible study, devotions, etc.) of growth, . . . the *degree* of the growth, . . . and the *effect* of the growth.

Scripture Study on Confession

IG Read Psalm 32:1-5.
What is the result of failing to confess your sins (vs. 3-4)? In what ways can you relate to this reality in your own life?
What is the result of honestly confessing to God (vs. 1-2, 5). Share examples of when you have experienced the joy of forgiveness.

IG 2. Read 1 John 1:7-10.
What happens when we try to pretend that our daily actions are beyond reproach (vs. 8, 10)? How confident can we be that the honest confession of our sins will be received by God (v. 9)? What is the basis for our forgiveness? (v. 7b)?

IG 3. Read Matthew 5:23 and James 5:16.
In what situations is it important for you to confess your sins to another person (Matthew 5:23)?
What activity is intended by God to be a part of the Christian fellowship? What promise accompanies it (James 5:16)?

IG 4. Read Ephesians 4:31-32.
Give examples of the wrong behavior which builds walls between people (v. 31). How can forgiveness help to break down those walls in a practical way (v. 32)?

Need for Confession in Marriage:

IG Discuss some recent situations in your home when confession was needed.

Roadblocks to Confession in Marriage

IG 1. Is it easier for you to confess a specific sin to your mate or to God? Why do you think that is so?

IG 2. In many marriages, one partner seems to assume the peacemaker's role. This is the partner that is first to say, "I'm sorry," and ask forgiveness from his/her mate for the sake of harmony. Do you think that you or your mate seems more willing and able to say, "I'm sorry"? Does this usually mean a genuine repentance or just a desire to end the fighting? Do you have other ways of showing you are sorry?

IG 3. "I'm sorry" is another way of saying, "Please forgive me." Yet often a mate doesn't respond to the "I'm sorry." A lack of response could be interpreted as a negative response such as "No, I do not forgive you." What is your normal response when your spouse says, "I'm sorry"? Do you have other ways besides words of showing you forgive your spouse? Why is it sometimes hard to forgive your spouse?

Personal Confesson Time with Spouse

PC 1. Couple Dialog and Confession Form (20—30 minutes)
Write: Areas where I have recently been falling short as a Christian husband/wife and how does it make me feel?

Couples then meet privately, exchange letters, share feelings, and use the form for Confession and Absolution printed in the introductory portion of this chapter.

IG 2. Share with the group your feelings about the private confessional time with your spouse. In what ways was it difficult? In what ways was it helpful?

IG 3. Closing group prayer around the circle along with reporting on prayer notebook requests and adding to the list.

ASSIGNMENT FOR SESSION 4

IG 1. Reread the Scripture sections for Session 3.

IG 2. Read the introductory material for Section II and Session 4.

IG 3. Prepare to report back on the use of "I'm sorry" and "I forgive you" during the time between group meetings.

IG 4. Continue to pray for the group's prayer requests.

SECTION II

Conflicts—Feelings and Issues

The Christian adventure of your couples' sharing group continues and accelerates the pace with this new section on "Conflicts—Feelings and Issues." Conflict resolution ranks as one of the top skills needed for a couple to enrich their marriage. Conflicts spring up in every marriage naturally and predictably because two separate people are joined together for everyday living. The conflicts can be healthy stepping stones to marital growth and a deeper relationship or serious stumbling blocks to a relationship that once seemed so smooth and serene.

This section will first give you an opportunity to examine three feelings which often surface in conflict situations. Sometimes they generate conflict situations. Failure to recognize the presence of these feelings in our own life and marriage can cause serious difficulty for our marriage. Failure to deal with these feelings constructively can tear apart the marriage relationship and harm us as persons. The three feelings in order of their discussion are guilt, anger, and jealousy.

Session 4 will feature an examination of guilt. You will explore the difference between guilt and a sense of guilt in your marriage relationship. You will identify specific areas of marriage where you feel guilty and recognize how you often try to impose guilt on your spouse. Before completing the session, you will help your spouse deal with guilty feelings in some practical ways.

Session 5 will tackle the subject of "Marriage and Dealing with Anger." You will learn to understand more clearly your own anger and the way you react to it. You will analyze the effects of anger upon your marriage and home. Finally, you will learn on the basis of Scripture to deal with anger more constructively as a way of deepening your marriage relationship.

Session 6 will zero in on "Marriage and Dealing with Jealousy." After exploring the effects of uncontrolled jealousy as a negative factor in our marriages, you will have an opportunity to deal with these negative effects by understanding and confessing its underlying causes. Finally, you will consider the positive effects of jealousy in the light of God as a "jealous God."

In Session 7 you will turn from the feelings surrounding conflict in marriage to the conflict issues which often arouse these feelings. You will evaluate conflicts in your marriage as to their subject matter and their intensity. You will then discuss positive and practical steps to deal with conflict issues in a more helpful and unifying manner. This session will prepare you for the next section, on "Conflict Resolution," which will present three areas where conflicts often arise—Special Days, Television, and Employment.

The four sessions in this section will be challenging to your group as you honestly discuss an important area of marital growth. You will find much common ground and similar struggles. You will need the Biblical message as your strength. Rich rewards await you as you face the feelings and issues surrounding conflict with the Spirit's gentle, guiding hand and the forgiving love of Jesus Christ.

CHAPTER 4

Marriage and Dealing with Guilt

Many conflicts in the home flare up because of guilt. In the first place, couples often disobey God's law and are guilty before Him. The list of sins could be endless: selfishness, sinful pride, resentment, bitterness, revenge, cutting remarks, jealousy, hatred, etc. Regular confession as outlined in the previous session is vital to a growing marriage. God has decisively handled all guilt and sin through the death of His Son Jesus Christ on the cross. We need not live under the burden of guilt because of God's grace in Christ.

Yet guilt continues to plague the marriage relationship. Satan, the accuser of the brethren, delights in stirring up constant guilt and anxiety. He also uses us to produce guilt in our spouse in order to get our own way. In short, all guilt is not the product of a godly conscience. We struggle with internal standards or dictums drummed into us by parents, friends, teachers, employers, and spouses which create a sense of guilt, not intended by God. ***Examples:*** "You should never make a mistake." "You must always be the best." "Losing is a disgrace." "Always have a spotless house." "Never spend money on yourself." "Don't openly show affection." "Work all the time. Recreation is frivolous." "Don't show your emotions. Keep a stiff upper lip." "Women are to stay at home and take care of the children." These are not God's clear commands but intentional or unintentional messages we have picked up from others.

In this session you will first explore the difference between guilt and a sense of guilt in your marriage relationship. Then you will have the chance to look over specific areas of your marriage where guilt is often produced. Each spouse will also be challenged to see how he/she imposes unnecesary guilt on the mate in order to gain some specific results. Finally, each couple will learn to help each other deal practically with guilt in the love and forgiveness of God.

GOALS FOR SESSION 4

1. Explore the difference between guilt and a sense of guilt
2. Identify specific areas in our marriage where we often feel guilty.
3. Recognize how we try to impose guilt upon our spouse to get results.
4. Help our spouse deal with guilty feelings in practical ways.

DEVOTIONAL THOUGHTS

Scripture

Romans 3:19; James 2:10—The reality of guilt before God.

Revelation 12:10—Satan as the creator of a sense of guilt
1 John 2:1-2—Christ as the one who deals with our guilt and the guilt of our spouse.
Philippians 2:1-4—Living together in grace, not guilt.

Group Prayer

GROUP EXERCISES

Getting Acquainted—Fellowship Prompter

IG Tell about an event in your life that brought you true fulfillment and inner peace.

Since We Last Met

IG Each person reports on any change in his/her use of "I'm sorry" and "I forgive you" since the last session. Try to include a specific example. Did the last session seem to have any effect on your hate? How?

Guilt and a Sense of Guilt

IG 1. Give an example of a time when you felt guilty

IG 2. Are there times when you feel a sense of guilt even though you are not actually guilty in God's eyes? If so, what causes you to feel guilty in those instances?

Specific Guilt-Producing Areas in Marriage

IG 1. Choose from the following list the items which frequently make you feel guilty and discuss your choices. Feel free to add additional items.

____ "I don't spend enough time with my mate."
____ "I'm too grouchy and irritable."
____ "I'm not good enough for him/her."
____ "I'm too messy in the house."
____ "I don't take good enough care of the children."
____ "I don't show enough thoughtfulness and love to my spouse."
____ "I don't communicate well with my spouse."
____ "I nag too much."
____ "I spend too much time at work."
____ "I embarrass my spouse in public."
____ "I watch too much television."

Imposing Guilt on Our Spouse

IG 1. In what ways do you try to impose guilt upon your spouse? How do you feel about such efforts? What might you do to stop imposing guilt?

Helping Our Spouse Deal with Guilt

PC 1. Personal Confession Time with Spouse: Confess any specific guilt brought to light by the discussion and absolve one another using the form printed in Chapter 3.

IG 2. Discuss with the group what you plan to do to help your spouse live more freely in grace, instead of in the bondage of guilt.

IG 3. Homework: Choose one guilt-producing area in your marriage and work on helping your spouse overcome the sense of guilt in specific ways before the next group meeting.

IG 4. Closing group prayer along with reporting on prayer notebook requests and adding to the list.

ASSIGNMENT FOR SESSION 5

IG 1. Reread the Scripture sections for Session 4.
IG 2. Read the introductory material for Session 5.
IG 3. Prepare to report back on your specific area of dealing with guilt.
IG 4. Continue to pray for the group's prayer requests.

CHAPTER 5

Marriage and Dealing with Anger

Most marital conflict involves anger. We have an explosive topic on our hands. Anger is a God-given emotion which is difficult to control. The Bible talks about the anger of God upon man's sin. A sinless Jesus expressed anger at the Pharisees and drove the money-changers out of the temple. Moses reacted with anger to the Israelite's idolatrous worship of a golden calf. Jonathan was angered by his father Saul's unjust treatment of David.

At the same time anger displayed by sinful human beings brought destruction throughout the pages of the Bible. Anger aroused Cain to kill his brother. Anger impelled Saul to throw his spear at David. Impulsively angry, Peter cut off the ear of the high priest's servant. The Bible condemns a hot temper and the rash actions accompanying such outbursts.

How is the Christian to view anger? How can anger be handled by the Christian couple? Is it wrong to be angry? What is the best way to express anger? Everyone feels anger at one time or another. Some repress the anger and bottle it up inside, only to find it causing serious emotional problems. Others suppress the expression of anger and seethe with resentment, bitterness, and a desire to get even. Still others vent their anger frequently without regard for the one who is hurt or what is said and done. Few people are able to express their anger constructively with a control and a love to communicate clearly and build up rather than tear down.

In this session you will have an opportunity first to understand your own anger more clearly and the ways you react to it. You will also be able to analyze the effects of anger upon your marriage and home.

Finally, you will use Scripture to guide you in dealing with anger more constructively. Confessing sins related to anger will be a part of this section.

Learning to deal with anger will provide an important key for good communication in marriage and for handling conflicts which naturally arise. As you better understand your own and your spouse's anger, you will find new ways to listen and care for one another when anger arises.

GOALS FOR SESSION 5

1. Learn to understand more clearly our anger and the way we react to it.
2. Analyze the effects of anger on our marriage and home.
3. Learn on the basis of Scripture to deal more constructively with our anger.

DEVOTIONAL THOUGHTS

Scripture

Mark 3:1-6—Jesus' legitimate anger (see Matthew 23 and John 2:13-17).
Genesis 4:5-8—Cain's sinful anger.
Ephesians 4:26-32—Right and wrong ways of dealing with anger.
Proverbs 14:29; 15:1, 18; 19:11—Expressing and receiving anger.

GROUP EXERCISES

Getting Acquainted—Fellowship Prompter

IG Describe what, in your opinion, was the happiest time you and your mate ever spent together.

Since We Last Met

IG Each person reports on any impact the last session has had in dealing with guilt. Be as specific as possible.

Understanding Anger and Our Reactions to It

IG 1. Describe exactly how you feel when you are really angry.
IG 2. Describe how you react when you are really angry.
IG 3. List and share some common causes of anger in your present life.

Analyzing the Effects of Anger in Our Home

IG 1. Try to recall and share a time when anger brought good results and a happy ending.

IG 2. *Wives only*—List and share several effects of an angry mother and wife on her family. *Husbands only*—List and share several effects of an angry father and husband on his family.
IG 3. In your experience what effects result from bottling up anger for an extended period of time?

Dealing with Anger Constructively

PC 1. Personal Confession Time with Spouse: During this special time confess to your mate your sins in dealing with anger. Hear your mate and forgive him/her as God has forgiven you.
IG 2. Reread the Scripture selections in the devotional thoughts and share brief reactions based on the discussion.
MC 3. After serious thought, tell the group specifically what you are going to do as a couple to deal with anger more effectively and lovingly.
IG 4. Closing group prayer along with reporting on prayer notebook requests and adding to the list.

ASSIGNMENT FOR SESSION 6

IG 1. Reread the Scripture sections for Session 5.
IG 2. Read the introductory material for Session 6.
IG 3. Prepare to report back on your experiences dealing with anger in your home between sessions.
IG 4. Continue to pray for the group's prayer requests.

CHAPTER 6

Marriage and Dealing with Jealousy

Many marriages break up because of an uncontrollable jealousy on the part of one or both spouses. Webster's dictionary defines "jealous" in its contemporary usage with these words:

> distrustful, suspicious, intolerant of rivalry, expecting exclusive devotion; disposed to suspect rivalry in matters of interest and affection; suspiciously watchful.

When one spouse views the other with constant jealousy, the other begins to feel mistrusted and unfairly smothered with suspicion and possessiveness. Uncontrolled jealousy seems to seethe and grow. Unchecked, it results in strife and fractured relationships. Jealousy is a real paradox because it normally affects only those we love, and sometimes the more we love, the more jealous we become. Jealousy seems to be rooted in the sins of greed and selfishness which make us overly possessive.

Ask yourself whether you feel jealous toward your spouse and if so, under what circumstances. How do you react when jealousy is directed at you? Do you feel flattered or do you rebel at the undue suspicion placed upon you? Is there a sense in which jealousy is good and contributes positively to a marriage?

Scripture presents jealousy in both a positive and a negative light. God refers to Himself as a jealous God, and St. Paul expresses godly jealousy for the Corinthian Christians who are wavering in their devotion to the true God. Webster lists an archaic definition of "jealous" that captures these positive ingredients—"zealous, devoted."

In this session you are given an opportunity to explore the negative aspects of jealousy in your marriage, to find ways to control these negative effects, and to build on the positive aspects of jealousy with God's help in the form of increased devotion to your spouse.

GOALS FOR SESSION 6

1. Explore the effects of uncontrolled jealousy as a negative factor in our marriage relationship.
2. Deal with the negative effects of jealousy by understanding and confessing its underlying causes.
3. Consider the positive effects of jealousy in the light of God as a "jealous God."

DEVOTIONAL THOUGHTS

Scripture

1 Corinthians 13:4—Love and jealousy.
Proverbs 6:34-35—Response of a jealous husband.
Genesis 37:3-4—Jealousy of Joseph's brothers.
Exodus 20:5-6—God as a jealous God.
2 Corinthians 11:1-4—Paul's godly jealousy for the Christians in Corinth.

Group Prayer

GROUP EXERCISES

Getting Acquainted—Fellowship Prompter

IG Describe the events that led to the time when you were "most proud of your mate."

Since We Last Met

IG Each person should attempt to share his experiences in dealing with anger in the home since the last session. Do you think you dealt with the anger more effectively and lovingly than usual? How?

The Effects of Uncontrolled Jealousy

IG 1. Do you think you or your mate is the more jealous? On what do you base your answers?

IG 2. Describe some actions that have surfaced as a result of your jealousy.

IG 3. *Wives only*—Many times husbands and fathers have been known to show jealousy regarding the attention you devote to your own children. What does this say to you?

IG 4. *Husbands only*—Many times wives have been known to show jealousy regarding your work, hobbies, and use of time. What does this say to you?

Dealing with Jealousy's Negative Effects

IG 1. What underlying attitudes cause you to be jealous in the negative sense?

PC 2. Personal Confession Time with Spouse: Use this time to confess any uncontrolled jealousy you may have. Hear your mate and forgive him/her as God has forgiven you.

Positive Effects of a Godly Jealousy

IG 1. In what sense does the Bible use jealousy as a positive quality? Note Exodus 20:5-6 and 2 Corinthians 11:1-4.

IG 2. Do you believe that a certain amount of jealousy in your mate is an expression of love and devotion to you? Describe what you believe to be the right amount of jealousy for your spouse to show towards you.

IG 3. Write a short love note to your mate using the word "love" several times. Then read the note to your mate but substitute "I'm jealous of" for each "love" word in the note. Thank your mate for loving you and being jealous of you.

Example:

My Dearest,

You know I love you very much. I loved you when we were first married, I love you right now, and I know I will love you even more tomorrow. I will always love you.

This would be converted to:

My Dearest,

You know I'm very jealous of you. I was jealous of you when we were first married, I'm jealous of you right now, and I know I will be jealous of you tomorrow. I will always be jealous of you.

IG Discuss with the group what you plan to do specifically to deal with the negative and positive aspects of jealousy in your relationship until the next session.

IG 5. Closing group prayer along with reporting on prayer notebook requests and adding to the list.

ASSIGNMENT FOR SESSION 7

IG 1. Reread the Scripture sections for Session 6.

IG 2. Read the introductory material for Session 7.

IG 3. Prepare to report back on your specific experiences of dealing with jealousy.

IG 4. Continue to pray for the group's prayer requests.

CHAPTER 7

Marriage and Dealing with Conflict Issues

So far in this section we have been focusing on the feelings which either cause conflict or are aroused by conflict—namely guilt, anger, and jealousy. When conflicts arise, we need to recognize and deal with the feelings stirred up. If we attempt to solve the conflict issues rationally without first recognizing the feelings involved, the situation may become worse. Sometimes the actual resolution of conflict needs to occur at a later time when hot feelings have cooled down.

Nevertheless, dealing with the actual conflict issues in a positive and useful way ranks as a high marriage priority. This session turns from an examination of the conflict feelings themselves to the conflict issues. We will look at the importance of putting two heads together for mutual solutions. You will have a chance to identify some of the issues in your marriage that generate conflict. You can then evaluate the way conflicts are currently being handled in your marriage.

Before the session is completed, you will be developing practical and positive steps to deal with conflict issues in a more helpful and unifying manner. The group will hold you accountable to report back on how you have progressed in handling conflict.

This session provides a stepping stone to the next section, on "Conflict Resolution." As you grow in your ability to identify and communicate your feelings in a conflict situation while listening to your spouse, and as you learn how to face the issues themselves in a mature and unselfish manner, you will have an opportunity to try out these skills by discussing the fairly "hot" topics of "Special Days," "Television," and "Employment."

Spend a little extra time with the Scripture sections for this lesson, understanding the two situations and how these conflict issues were approached. They should provide some helpful thoughts as you evaluate conflict issues in your own marriage.

GOALS FOR SESSION 7

1. Evaluate conflicts in our marriage, observing both the decisions that have brought us closer and the issues which frequently divide us.
2. Take positive and practical steps to deal with conflict issues in a more helpful and unifying manner.

DEVOTIONAL THOUGHTS

Scripture

1 Corinthians 3:1-9—What conflict existed in the Corinthian church (3:1-4)? (See also 1:10-13.) How does Paul try to help them resolve this conflict (3:3-9)?

Acts 15:1-35—What conflict arose between Paul and the Judaizers (vs. 1-2)? How did Paul and Barnabas seek to resolve the matter (vs. 2-5)? what role did James play in resolving the conflict (vs. 12-21)? How was the conflict finally resolved (vs. 22-29)?

Group Prayer

GROUP EXERCISES

Getting Acquainted—Fellowship Prompter

IG Describe in detail what has been your "life's most embarrassing moment."

Since We Last Met

IG Have you had an opportunity to deal with jealousy since the last session?
If possible, share an actual experience and how you handled your jealousy.

Evaluating Conflicts in Our Marriage

IG 1. "Two heads are better than one" states the old adage. The important and often heavy decisions required in a marriage as well as the unique mutual marital relationship brings this adage into nearly daily use in our lives. List and share with the group two or three major decisions of your married life where the support and agreement of your spouse really served to reinforce you. Examples could include choosing your present living quarters—the school your children attend—your job, etc.

IG 2. What are some of the issues that seem to cause conflict in your marriage? Describe briefly.

IG 3. As the husband and wife serve as the two heads of marriage sharing and discussing their own ideas and reasonings, a degree of conflict is as natural as tomorrow's sunrise. It is the frequency, depth of the conflict, and the manner of resolution that makes this conflict helpful or harmful. Choose one phrase from each of the following three groups to form a sentence that most nearly describes how you see conflict in your marriage:

1

It seems we always disagree
We often disagree
We sometimes disagree
We seldom disagree
We never disagree

2

and end up in a bitter argument
and have a little quarrel
and have a spat
to the point of hurt feelings
because we are so much alike

3

and stay angry for a long time.
but it seems (I-he-she) always wins.
but it doesn't last long.
but we always settle it.
and we are always both happy at the end.

Were you surprised at the sentence your mate used? Why or why not?

Steps for Dealing with Conflict Issues

IG 1. Since some conflict is not only natural, but actually healthy for a good marriage, we should make every effort to use our conflicts in a mature, growing, and positive manner. Choose three of the listed helps in order of importance to you that you believe would most help the two of you to make the best use of your conflicts. Share your answers and reasons.

a. Make some rules for disagreeing.
b. Stop and pray for guidance.
c. Postpone the discussion until the two of you are alone.
d. Ask for others' opinions.
e. Maintain an open mind.
f. Be determined that something good is going to come from this.
g. Always finish the discussion with a kiss.
h. "Sleep on it."
i. Anything that you believe would be truly helpful.

MC 2. Husbands and wives should spend about 10 minutes together to develop a statement for the group about how and what they have agreed to do in order to make the conflicts of their marriage into a more useful and positive experience. Typical statements may be:

a. We realize that if we both sit down, stay cool, and intelligently discuss our opinions, we will make a good decision.
b. We have agreed always to settle our differences before we go to bed.
c. We have agreed to disagree in a Christian manner.

PC 3. Personal Confession Time with Spouse: Make use of this special time to confess your shortcomings in your conflicts and their resolutions.

IG 4. Share briefly with the group your specific plan for making conflicts more useful and positive.

IG 5. Closing Group Prayer along with reporting on prayer notebook requests and adding to the list.

ASSIGNMENT FOR SESSION 8

IG 1. Reread the Scripture sections for Session 7, thinking of your own conflict areas.
IG 2. Read the introductory material for Session 8.
IG 3. Prepare to report back on your specific steps for dealing with conflict issues.
IG 4. Continue to pray for the group's prayer requests.

SECTION III

Conflict Resolution

Unresolved conflicts create problems for any marriage. But facing conflict areas thoughtfully and lovingly can add a very positive dimension to your marriage. In this section we have selected three topics which often generate conflict for a husband and wife—special days, television, and employment. Your group is invited to tackle these intensely relevant subjects on the basis of the skills gained in the previous section. You have sensitized yourselves to a better understanding of feelings aroused in a conflict situation (Chapters 4—6), and you have worked on some ideas for resolving conflict issues (Chapter 7). Now as you discuss these three potentially controversial subjects, listen carefully to your spouse's feelings while communicating your own feelings in a nonthreatening way. Then work on practical steps for dealing with the conflict issues to your mutual satisfaction.

Session 8 features a discussion of "Marriage and Special Days." You will survey and rank in importance for your family the traditional holidays and personal times which occur each year. In the process of learning your own preferences and dislikes, you will identify which special days cause the greatest conflicts for your marriage. Together you will confess the problems and draft an approach for resolving the conflict on at least one special day.

Session 9 brings you face to face with "Marriage and Television." Because television occupies such a prominent place in most homes and affects the lives of all the family members directly or indirectly, it can easily become a storm center for marital controversy. In this session you will do some survey thinking about television viewing habits in your home. Then you will attempt to isolate the specific conflicts in your marriage generated by television. Finally, you will try to resolve these conflicts by developing an experimental plan for disciplined television viewing.

Session 10 directs your attention to the potential conflicts between "Marriage and Employment." The demands of a husband's employment have for years presented a possible strain on the marriage relationship. But in recent times the huge increase of working wives has created new conflicts between husbands and wives. This session will give you a chance to explore your own and your spouse's current feelings about employment. You will then identify the specific marital conflicts created by your employment and that of your spouse. Once again you will sit down together and develop a plan for resolving some of these work-related marriage conflicts.

A spirited and honest group discussion of these three areas should provide each couple with a better understanding of current feelings, a beginning step towrd conflict resolution in each of the areas, and a foundation for continued home sharing on these issues for a long time to come. The Scriptural material should be faithfully studied to give you solid Christ-centered moorings for your group discussions.

CHAPTER 8

Marriage and Special Days

Every family celebrates certain special days each year. Some are unique to your own family such as birthdays, vacations, or personal outings. Others are common to all Christians, to your community, to your nation or even to the world. Examples would include Christmas, Easter, Thanksgiving, July 4th, Memorial Day, etc. All of these days are supposed to be joyful and meaningful celebrations which draw you closer as a Christian family.

Unfortunately, special days often provide a battleground for serious conflicts in marriage. Separate traditions from childhood sometimes clash in the new home. Relatives and their plans for your celebration of special days often create tension on your marriage. Husband and wife frequently have widely different expectations for how the holiday should be spent. Children at times dominate the special day and eliminate time alone for the couple.

Special days can be a rose to one side of the marriage and a thorn to the other. Can Christmas be as special to a wife who is nearly exhausted from shopping, decorating, cleaning, and cooking (with the children at home instead of at school) as it is to the husband who, relatively speaking, can enjoy the gradual buildup of excitement and enthusiasm for the day which celebrates the birth of Christ? Can a vacation trip be as special to a husband who has to drive, make reservations, and endure extra efforts and worries as it is to the wife who does not have to shoulder these extra responsibilities? The answer to those questions is probably "no," but we believe that a better understanding of these special days from each partner's perspective will greatly help.

In this session, you will first survey special days of the year and rank them in order of importance to your family. Then you will identify those days which cause the greatest conflict. The group will help you develop practical ways to resolve the conflicts.

GOALS FOR SESSION 8

1. Survey special days of the year for our family and rank in order of importance.
2. Identify those special days causing the greatest conflict and openly discuss the problems.
3. Anticipate practical ways to resolve these conflicts.

DEVOTIONAL THOUGHTS

Scripture

Luke 2:41-52—What special days were being observed by the Holy Family? What problem developed on the way home? How do you think they were affected by the conflict?

2 Samuel 6:12-23—What special day was David celebrating? How did he choose to celebrate? What effect did his celebration have on his wife Michael? How was the conflict handled?

Group Prayer

GROUP EXERCISES

Getting Acquainted—Fellowship Prompter

IG Talk about the best joke you have ever pulled on your mate.

Since We Last Met

IG Each person reports on a specific incident of conflict that occurred since the last session and how it was dealt with. As you look back on the incident, are you now pleased with the manner in which it was resolved?

A Survey of Special Days

IG 1. Rank the following special days starting with No. 1 as the most special to you. Add any days that are special to you but are not on the list and place them in the proper order or priority. Then share your rankings with the group.

Family birthdays	_____	Veterans' Day	_____
Christmas	_____	Labor Day	_____
Easter	_____	Memorial Day	_____
Thanksgiving	_____	New Year's Eve	_____
Family vacations	_____	New Year's Day	_____
Personal days (fishing, shopping, etc., where only one is involved)	_____	Baptismal birthdays	_____
		Wedding anniversaries	_____
July 4th	_____		

IG 2. Share with the group your reasons for choosing your top five choices above. Exactly what do these days mean to you, and why are they so special to you?

Special Days Creating Conflict

IG 1. Find the one special day on the list that has the greatest difference in ranking between each husband and wife in the group. Explain to the group your reasons for such a high or low ranking and make a special effort to listen to your mate's explanation.

IG 2. Find the one special day on the list that has the smallest difference in ranking for each couple. Explain to the group why the two of you agree in either liking or disliking the special day chosen.

IG 3. On special days do you conform to certain traditions which you find very distasteful? What are some changes you would like to make?

Resolving Conflicts on Special Days

PC 1. Personal Confession Time with Spouse—Confess to each other your own failures in celebrating special days and any of your wrong attitudes toward your spouse's feelings about special days. Offer God's forgiveness to your spouse.

MC As a couple, choose one special day for the coming year where there has been conflict. Discuss what each of you can and will do to make that day more enjoyable for your mate. Indicate your intentions to the group and report back after the special day passes.

IG 3. Closing group prayer along with reporting on prayer notebook requests and adding to the list.

ASSIGNMENT FOR SESSION 9

IG 1. Reread the Scripture sections for Session 8.
IG 2. Read the introductory material for Session 9.
IG 3. Prepare to report back on your thoughts and plans about special days.
IG 4. Continue to pray for the group's prayer request.

CHAPTER 9

Marriage and Television

How does television affect your marriage? Forty years ago the question would never have been asked. But no course on marriage can easily avoid the subject of television as a profound influence on the modern home. Television itself is a gift of God's creation with great potential for good. It can also be used as a tool of Satan to cause much harm and instill the world's wrong values.

The topic is much larger than can be covered in a single session. This session will give you an opportunity to think broadly about the many implications of television for your home. Then the questions will zero in on television as a source of potential conflict in your marriage. You will be able to analyze how your own viewing affects your marital relationship and learn how your spouse views the importance and problems of television for the family. The group discussion will no doubt reveal the wide variety of attitudes, preferences, and values concerning television viewing.

After some private confession time with your spouse, you will spend time in developing a plan for disciplined viewing of television to be implemented between sessions. This practical plan should help you to formulate and apply your own Christian values as a couple in the area of television viewing. The result should be a reduction of conflict over television in your home.

Use this session as an introduction to the discussion of television values in your home. Continue the process at home, also involving your children. Give feedback to the group at your next meeting and occasionally make reference to your progress and/or problems in subsequent sessions. God will bless your efforts to honor Him in your positive use of disciplined television viewing.

GOALS FOR SESSION 9

1. Do some reflective thinking about the whole area of television viewing in our home.
2. Recognize and discuss specific conflicts in our marriage which arise over television viewing.
3. Develop as a way of resolving conflict an experimental plan for a short period of time to discipline our use of television.

DEVOTIONAL THOUGHTS:

Scripture

Nehemiah 9:6, 13-17—Thanksgiving for God's creation and the reality of sin against God's law. (This provides a background for thinking of television as a gift of God's creation that can be used properly or abused.)

Ephesians 5:15-20—Guidelines for a disciplined viewing of television to God's glory.

Group Prayer

GROUP EXERCISES

Getting Acquainted—Fellowship Prompter

IG Which is the happiest room in your house, and what do you think makes it so?

Since We Last Met

IG Each person shares any new thoughts or plans which the last session prompted insofar as special days are concerned.

Thinking About Television in Your Home

IG 1. Quickie questions. Each person should answer the following questions in just a few words each with no explanations or discussion.

a. How many TV sets are operative in your home?
b. About how many hours do you watch TV on an average Wednesday?
c. About how many hours do you normally watch TV a week?
d. Who in your home normally turns the TV on?
e. Who in your home normally turns the TV off?
f. What do you truly think about the quality of the programs?
g. Do you regularly watch TV news?
h. Do you regularly watch TV sports?
i. Do you normally watch TV soap operas?
j. What is your favorite regular show?
k. Does TV interfere with your family meal time?
l. Does TV interfere with your normal bedtime?
m. Do you think you watch too much TV?
n. Do you think your mate watches too much TV?
o. Do you think your children watch too much TV?
p. Who, if anyone, screens and approves the programs for family viewing?
q. Do you use TV as a "babysitter"?
r. Do you think TV is a source of conflict in your home?

IG 2. TV has the capability of being a tremendous educational and entertainment influence on your family in a positive way. What changes would you have to make in your viewing habits to take advantage of this capability?

IG 3. TV has been blamed for many of the ills in our present society including the increase of violence. Do you personally believe this to be true? Do you give the TV in your home opportunities to be such a negative influence on your family?

Marriage Conflicts over Television

IG 1. Has TV ever caused an argument or disagreement between you and your mate? Can you recall such an occurrence in the recent past? What changes would be necessary to prevent this same disagreement in the future?

IG 2. It would seem that we need to apply different levels of discipline in our viewing as our audience changes. What type of TV discipline do you think should be applied in the following situations?

a. When only you are viewing?
b. When only your children are viewing?
c. When the whole family is viewing?
d. When only the two of you are viewing?
e. When you have expected guests?
f. When you have unexpected guests?

Resolving Conflicts Created by Television

PC 1. Personal Confession Time with Spouse: Confess and absolve one another in the area of conflicts because of television viewing in your home.

IG 2. Rules for viewing TV are difficult to establish because of all the variables. It would appear that this could be an area where "common sense" needs to apply; yet common sense areas are destined to bring out the vast differences in discipline, values, etc. that sometimes make up a marriage. Everyone agrees that we go on green and stop on red, but can we agree on what is suitable material for TV viewing in a given family situation? Use the next 15 minutes to think and write notes about the TV viewing in your home. Jot down changes that could be made that would have avoided past controversies and hopefully will help you to avoid controversies over TV viewing in the future. These changes should be in the form of what *you are willing to do rather than what your spouse should do!* Share these thoughts with your group.

MC 3. Do you truly believe that TV viewing is a source of conflict or an area of your life that needs improvement? Would you be willing to try a day or even a week of disciplined TV viewing? With your spouse, select a time and in general agree in your viewing for that period of time. Give it a try and report the results back to your group.

IG 4. Closing group prayer along with reporting on prayer notebooks requests and adding to the list.

ASSIGNMENT FOR SESSION 10

IG 1. Reread the Scripture sections for Session 9.
IG 2. Read the introductory material for Session 10.
IG 3. Prepare to report back on your "disciplined TV viewing experiment."
IG 4. Continue to pray for the group's prayer requests.

CHAPTER 10

Marriage and Employment

How does your employment affect your marriage? That is the central question of Session 10. "If any would not work, neither should he eat," the Bible tells us. God placed us on earth to work for His glory. Whether paid or not paid, every husband and wife spends many hours each week working. A number of questions arise in our modern society regarding employment and the marriage relationship:

Is employment available to support the family? Is the husband happy with his job? Does he have goals for the future? How much time does he need to spend at work either for loyalty to the company, money, or advancement? Will the wife work? If so, how much? What are her reasons for working—needed money, personal fulfillment, desire to contribute to society, escape from the home, etc? If the wife works, how does her job, earning power, and time spent affect the husband and the home? How much time is spent by husband and wife in discussing employment—too little, too much? Does each spouse truly understand and support the feelings of the other regarding employment?

In this session you will first have an opportunity to verbalize your own feelings on employment and listen closely to the feelings of your spouse. You will also identify the touchy areas of employment which create conflict between yourself and your spouse. Finally, you will work on ways to communicate better and resolve some of these conflict areas.

Try to place your discussion of this topic in the light of God's plan for work and His overall purposes for your life in terms of love and service to Him and others, beginning with your spouse and family. View this topic as an ongoing concern which requires careful thought, listening, and planning. God intends a harmonious relationship between your employment and your marriage. Seek His unique direction for your home.

GOALS FOR SESSION 10

1. Explore our own and our spouse's feelings about employment.
2. Identify the specific marital conflicts created by our employment and that of our spouse.
3. Work on specific ways to resolve this conflict.

DEVOTIONAL THOUGHTS

Scripture

Genesis 2:15; 3:19—God's intentions for work; the results of the fall into sin on work.
2 Thessalonians 3:10-13—Faithful work commanded instead of idleness.
Ecclesiastes 2:11—Vanity of our human labor.
John 6:27—Work in the light of eternal life.

Group Prayer

GROUP EXERCISES

Getting Acquainted—Fellowship Prompter

IG Tell about the craziest thing you ever did.

Since We Last Met

IG Did you really try a "disciplined TV viewing" experiment? If not, why not, and do you ever intend to try? If yes, how did it work?

Exploring Feelings About Employment

IG 1. Are you satisfied with your job? Your spouse's?

IG 2. Just how important do you think the subject of employment is in the makeup of a good marriage?

IG 3. Rate the following from 1 to 10, marking as number 1 the most important in your overall assessment of your own employment. Share your answers with the group. Explain as needed.

a. Pay scale ______
b. Hours ______
c. Fringe benefits ______
d. Reputation of employer ______
e. Immediate supervisor ______
f. Fellow workers ______
g. Location ______
h. Sense of accomplishment ______
i. Opportunity to advance ______
j. Retirement plan ______

IG 4. What are your sincere ambitions in your employment?

IG 5. Do you make an effort to involve and talk about your workday with your mate? How and how much?

IG 6. As we discuss employment, we must also consider vacations as an integral part of the total employment picture.

a. How important are vacations to you?
b. What, for you, would be a "perfect" vacation"?
c. About how much vacation time do you need to be really effective at your work?
d. Vacations serve to rest and relax us, but they are also intended to "refuel" us for our job. Have your recent vacations served both purposes? Why and how?

Employment as a Source of Marital Conflict

IG 1. What area of the husband's employment causes the greatest conflict in your home and why? See question three in "Exploring Feelings" for possible conflict areas. Other conflict areas might include unemployment, dissatisfaction with work, over-involvement in work, or bringing home your work problems.

IG 2. What aspect of the wife's employment or not being employed causes the greatest conflict in your home and why?

PC 3. Personal Confession Time with Spouse: Spend time confessing your own wrong attitudes toward employment and failure to understand your spouse's feelings on the subject. Absolve each other with Christ's forgiveness.

Resolving Marital Conflicts on Employment

IG 1. Name some specific ways you could be more supportive of your spouse and his/her employment. Tell the group and hold yourself accountable for a report back to them.

IG 2. Do you believe any benefits would be derived from sitting down together at least twice a year and discussing your job? If so, exactly what would you talk about?

IG 3. Closing Group prayer along with reporting on prayer notebook requests and adding to the list. Thank God for your employment and ask Him to continue to guide you in this area.

ASSIGNMENT FOR SESSION 11

IG 1. Reread the Scripture sections for Session 10.

IG 2. Read the introductory material for Session 11.

IG 3. Prepare to report back on your efforts to lessen marital conflicts on the subject of employment.

IG 4. Continue to pray for the group's prayer requests. Make it a practice to thank God regularly for your employment and to ask Him for guidance.

SECTION IV

Moving On

We started our Christian adventure with a section on "Going with God." You made new commitments to your spouse, to your group, and to God. You looked at the need for Christian maturity personally, spiritually, and in your marriage. You took an in-depth look at confession as a vital, practical, and Biblical tool for your marriage. Throughout the course, you have learned the skill and the attitude of honest confession with your spouse.

Your group next encountered a section on "Conflicts—Feelings and Issues." You were willing to probe the uncomfortable feeling of guilt, anger, and jealousy with a patient listening to one another and a sometimes painful sharing of how conflict situations trigger these emotions in yourself and in your marriage. You then developed an approach for dealing with conflict issues which often remain even after the feelings have been therapeutically expressed.

Most recently your group had a chance to practice your conflict resolution skills on three intensely practical subjects in the modern home. Special days were explored for conflict-producing situations. Television was surveyed with its enormous impact on many families, and again conflict areas were identified. Finally, the subject of employment was discussed as it affects both husbands and wives. Conflicts also surfaced because of job-related problems.

Now the book concludes with three sessions on "Moving On." "Marriage and the Life Cycle" will emphasize that your marriage needs to continually grow as you move from one stage in life to the next. The effects of your children's development also profoundly influence your marriage.

Your marriage needs a strong commitment to regular Bible Study personally, in your marriage, and in group settings. You will have an opportunity to evaluate your use of the Bible and make specific plans for improving in this vital area.

The final session, "Marriage and the Future," will enable you to evaluate this course for your group and to look to the future. You will also look at your marriage in terms of short-range and long-range growth. Hopefully, you will decide to continue Christ-centered and Bible-based growth for your marriage in a Christian small group setting. "Moving On" with the Lord, your spouse, and a group of caring Christian couples, your Christian adventure through life can continue in new and exciting opportunities for love and service.

CHAPTER 11

Marriage and the Life Cycle

This final section, entitled "Moving On," begins with a session on "Marriage and the Life Cycle." Our life never stands still. The years roll on like a rushing river . . . birth, infancy, childhood, adolescence, young adulthood, middle age, old age, death. In our youth we think we will live forever with time moving slowly. As we age, time seems to accelerate. Each stage of our life cycle brings certain changes in our viewpoints, goals, experiences, needs, and problems.

Marriage is definitely affected by the different stages of the life cycle. Newlyweds without children have different needs and problems than do middle-aged couples with teenage children. Wives with children in diapers requiring constant attention certainly struggle with a different burden than wives who look at an empty nest with the children grown and wonder what their purpose in life is now. Husbands who are struggling to build a career and earn enough money to buy a home face different challenges from husbands who have reached their job peak and are tapering off toward retirement.

In this session each of you will reflect on your particular stage in the life cycle relative to where you have been and where you are headed. You will examine how these changes are affecting your marriage. The diversity of the group and/or the similarities should be quite helpful in thinking through the life cycle. Then you will specifically look at the effects of your children's different stages of development on your marriage.

Looking ahead, you will examine your feelings and plans regarding old age and death. Are you looking forward to the later years? Are you prepared for your own death or the death of your spouse? Finally, you will together appropriate God's resources in Christ for your marriage in the various stages of the life cycle. He promises to be with us in every situation. He has a plan for our lives which gives purpose to each day and which extends beyond the grave to an eternity of praise before the throne of the Lamb.

GOALS FOR SESSION 11

1. Reflect on our own life cycle and how our marriage has been affected by the passing years.
2. Consider the effect of our children's developmental stages on our marriage.
3. Examine our feelings and plans regarding old age and death.
4. Appropriate God's resources for our marriage in the various stages of our life cycle.

DEVOTIONAL THOUGHTS

Scripture

Psalm 90—The rapid passage of time in our lives and a prescription for using God's resources.

Ecclesiastes 3:1-15—A time for everything in God's plan.

1 Timothy 4:12—5:4—Interaction in the church between different ages in the life cycle.

Group Prayer

GROUP EXERCISES

Getting Acquainted—Fellowship Prompter

IG Tell about a happening in your married life when your mate made you feel most loved and cherished.

Since We Last Met

IG Each person share any new thoughts and plans to lessen marital conflict in your home related to the subject of employment.

Reflections on Your Life Cycle

IG 1. Divide your life into 10-year age spans . . . 1 to 10 years of age; 10—20; 20—30, and so on. Share with the group the one or two major events in each of the periods.

IG 2. Share your thoughts on each of the following with your marriage in mind:

a. Today is the best day of my life.
b. The best age of life is my age.
c. The older I get the faster time seems to pass.
d. I really look forward to the future.
e. If I had it to do over again, I'd probably do it the same way.

Children and the Life Cycle

IG 1. What are the effects of children on the marriage and the lives of parents during the following age spans?

a. Infant and toddler years
b. Preteen years
c. Teen years
d. After the youngest child has left home.

PC 2. Personal Confession Time with Spouse: Confess your shortcomings relative to your children's development and the life-cycle needs of your spouse. Affirm God's forgiveness in Christ to your spouse.

Looking Toward Old Age and Death

IG 1. Share some of your plans and dreams for your senior years.

IG 2. Share some of your thoughts on each of the following:

a. Is death a difficult subject for you and your spouse to discuss?
b. Have you done anything to prepare your mate for your eventual death?
c. Which member of your marriage do you believe would be best able to cope alone?
d. As of today, do you consider "your affairs to be in order"? If not, what needs to be done and when do you plan to do it?

God's Resources for Your Marriage in the Life Cycle

IG 1. Read and meditate on Psalm 23. God has said He will be with us—now and always. Does this give you the confidence and joy to face the future of the rest of your life and all eternity? Are you willing to grasp the loving hand of Jesus Christ and let Him lead you? Share your thoughts on your present relationship to Jesus and your future plans for that relationship. Continue your life-cycle discussion between sessions.

IG 2. Closing group prayer along with reporting on prayer notebook requests and adding to the list.

ASSIGNMENT FOR SESSION 12

IG 1. Reread the Scripture sections for Session 11.
IG 2. Read the introductory materials for Session 12.
IG 3. Prepare to report back on what you learned from this session and your interim discussions on the life cycle.
IG 4. Continue to pray for the group's prayer requests.

CHAPTER 12

Marriage and the Bible

What place does the Bible have in your own life and in your marriage? As Christians we affirm the Bible as the inspired Word of God, pointing to Jesus Christ as the Savior of the world. We insist that the Word of God be preached and taught in its truth and purity. But do you *use* the Bible on a daily basis as a source of strength, comfort, and guidance? Or does your Bible gather dust on the shelf?

This session is designed to help you take stock of your personal Bible habits, including it's use in your marriage. Together your group can honestly share the good experiences of Bible study as well as the disappointing ones. You can reflect on your use or nonuse of the Bible in worship, in formal group Bible study, in small informal groups, in your family devotions, in your time as a couple, and in your personal devotional time. You can also identify what roadblocks seem to stand in the way of consistent and meaningful Bible study. Your problems may well be shared by others in the group. Your helpful insights may stimulate thinking in the other group members.

You will look at some Scripture passages that will present God's directives and promises regarding the use of His Word. This Scripture study should help provide some objectivity and purpose for developing a specific Bible plan. After confessing to your spouse, you will have an opportunity to devise some action steps. Your plan between sessions should be achievable and practical. Your group will hold you accountable for what you decide to do.

No topic could make God happier than this one. As you determine to strengthen your relationship to the living Word of God, the Holy Spirit will mightily empower you to grow and apply the Good News of Jesus to every area of life, including your marriage and family relationships.

GOALS FOR SESSION 12

1. Take stock of our own personal Bible study in all settings, including its use in our marriage.
2. Look at Scripture passages which stress the importance of Bible study.

3. Develop with our spouse a specific Bible plan to increase meaningful Bible study in our lives.

DEVOTIONAL THOUGHTS

Scripture

Isaiah 55:1-3—God's thirst-quenching and life-giving Word.
1 Peter 1:23—2:3—God's Word as enduring Good News and spiritual milk.
2 Timothy 3:14-17—God's Word as reliable and practical for daily living.

Group Prayer

GROUP EXERCISES

Getting Acquainted—Fellowship Prompter

IG Describe a famous person who most reminds you of your mate and say why.

Since We Last Met

IG Each person shares thoughts and reflections that were prompted by the last session on the life cycle.

Taking Stock of Our Bible Study

IG 1. The Bible . . . the Word of God . . .
- a. How many Bibles do you have in your home?
- b. Which versions?
- c. Which is your favorite?
- d. About how long do you spend with your Bible in your average week?

IG 2. About what percentage of your total weekly Bible time is spent
- a. In personal reading and meditation?
- b. In group study?
- c. In worship?
- d. Other (please specify)?

IG 3. What priority do you put on personal Bible Study? What priority do you believe it should have?

IG 4. What influence did you have from your parents, teachers, and friends during your preadult years relative to Bible study?

IG 5. What influence do you consider yourself to be on your mate and/or children relative to Bible study now?

IG 6. Give examples of reading the Bible in these areas.
- a. For study
- b. For pleasure
- c. For comfort
- d. For thanksgiving
- e. For reference

IG 7. What is the best way for you to select your Bible reading?
- a. By need
- b. By book
- c. By continuation of cover to cover

d. By hit and miss
e. By assignment
f. As a result of prayerful inspiration
g. Other

IG 8. What are the one or two biggest deterrents that prevent you from spending a portion of your daily time with your Bible? Are these insurmountable deterrents or could they be overcome?

Listening to Scripture on Bible Study

IG 1. Reread the three passages used in the opening devotion. What do they have to say about the importance of Bible study?

IG 2. Read *Matthew 4:1-11*. How did Jesus use the Word of God when tempted by Satan? See *Ephesians 6:10-17*. What implications can you draw for our use of God's Word to prepare for temptation?

IG 3. Read *Colossians 3:16-17; Matthew 13:1-9, 18-23*—According to these passages how important is the regular, disciplined study of God's Word?

PC 4. Personal Confession Time with Spouse: In the light of your Bible study evaluation and the above passages, confess to each other your failures in Bible study and attitudes. Announce to each other the full forgiveness of Jesus Christ.

Developing a Specific Bible Study Plan

IG 1. Do you truly want to improve your Bible study time? Are you willing to do something about it? Answer only yes or no.

MC 2. Right now, with your spouse, design a workable/achievable plan for Bible study for the interval until your next group meeting. Specify the time, amount of time, and the day when the two of you will read and study the Bible together. State your plan to your group and ask them not only to encourage you and pray for you, but also to hold you accountable to reach your goal and report back.

IG 3. Closing prayer along with reporting on prayer notebook requests and adding to the prayer list.

ASSIGNMENT FOR SESSION 13

IG 1. Reread the Scripture sections for Session 12.
IG 2. Read the introductory material for Session 13.
IG 3. Prepare to report back on the progress of your Bible study plan.
IG 4. Continue to pray for the group's prayer requests.

CHAPTER 13

Marriage and the Future

This is the final meeting of our thirteen-session Christian adventure together. All good things come to an end, and we all need to be "moving on." You will have a chance in this session to evaluate the course and the group experience and to look to the future.

Answer the following questions: In what ways has the group been meaningful to you and your spouse? What have you learned about yourself, your spouse, and the group? Do you want the group sessions to continue? Or would you like to disband? Do you want to continue with the same group members, or divide up and each couple form a new group with additional couples? If you continue, what materials do you plan to use and what format will you follow? Work closely with your pastor in these decisions. He may have other marriage enrichment or small group materials to suggest to you.

In this session you will also have a chance to sit down with your spouse and make some short-range and long-range plans for your future based on the topics covered in this book. The group will then thank each member for helping encourage marriage growth and thank God for His love and mercy in Christ.

You have now made a significant beginning in the area of marriage enrichment. We continue as regular members of our own small groups because we believe that God wants us to grow each day in our marriage and in our relationship to God. The Christian couple's group provides us with a supportive atmosphere to keep us centered on our goals and depending on Jesus Christ for growth and healing in our marriages

GOALS FOR SESSION 13

1. Evaluate the course and the group experience.
2. Discuss the future for this group.
3. Discuss as a couple the future for our marriage.
4. Thank and affirm each of the group members for their Christian ministry to us.

DEVOTIONAL THOUGHTS

Scripture

Acts 2:31-47—The importance of Christians ministering to one another in small groups with the Word as their focus.

Philippians 3:12-14—The importance of continuing to grow in the Christian life as individuals and as couples.

Group Prayer

GROUP EXERCISES

Getting Acquainted—Fellowship Prompter

IG Describe what, in your mind's eye, you perceive yourself to be 20 years from now—both physically and otherwise.

Since We Last Met

IG Each person shares with the group the progress of his Bible study plan.

Evaluating the Course and Planning the Group's Future

IG 1. Take a few minutes and evaluate the worth of this course and this group on your marriage and your life.

IG 2. What do you personally want to see as a future for this group?

IG 3. Suggest specific ideas for followup materials if the group plans to continue.

Future for Our Marriage

IG 1. Personal Time with Spouse—Spend some time developing short-range and long-range plans for your marriage which build on the topics of this course.

IG 2. Group Discussion: What do you personally want to see as a future for your marriage?

IG 3. Support . . . love . . . confidence . . . joy and happiness . . . plus all the other necessary ingredients for a fulfilling life and marriage are all available to you in abundance from God our Father and from those that love you. Take this opportunity to thank each of the contributors personally for what they have meant to you and the group.

IG 4. You are truly a wonderfully made creature that God loves very much just the way you are. Let your light shine and let your love for each other grow and be strengthened that your lives together here might approach the pure joy and happiness that you know you have in life eternal with Jesus Christ. Use this opportunity to thank and praise God for what He means to you and the group. Include closing group prayer as part of your praise.